Dear Reader,

Our stories are inspired by time spent together as a family. Whether camping outside in our kids' tree fort, hiking in the mountains, or snorkeling in the ocean; my family and I have enjoyed some wonderful moments and amazing adventures over the years.

When you read *Anthony's Outdoor Adventure* with the children in your life, my hope is that the story takes you back to your own childhood memories and the simple joys of being young.

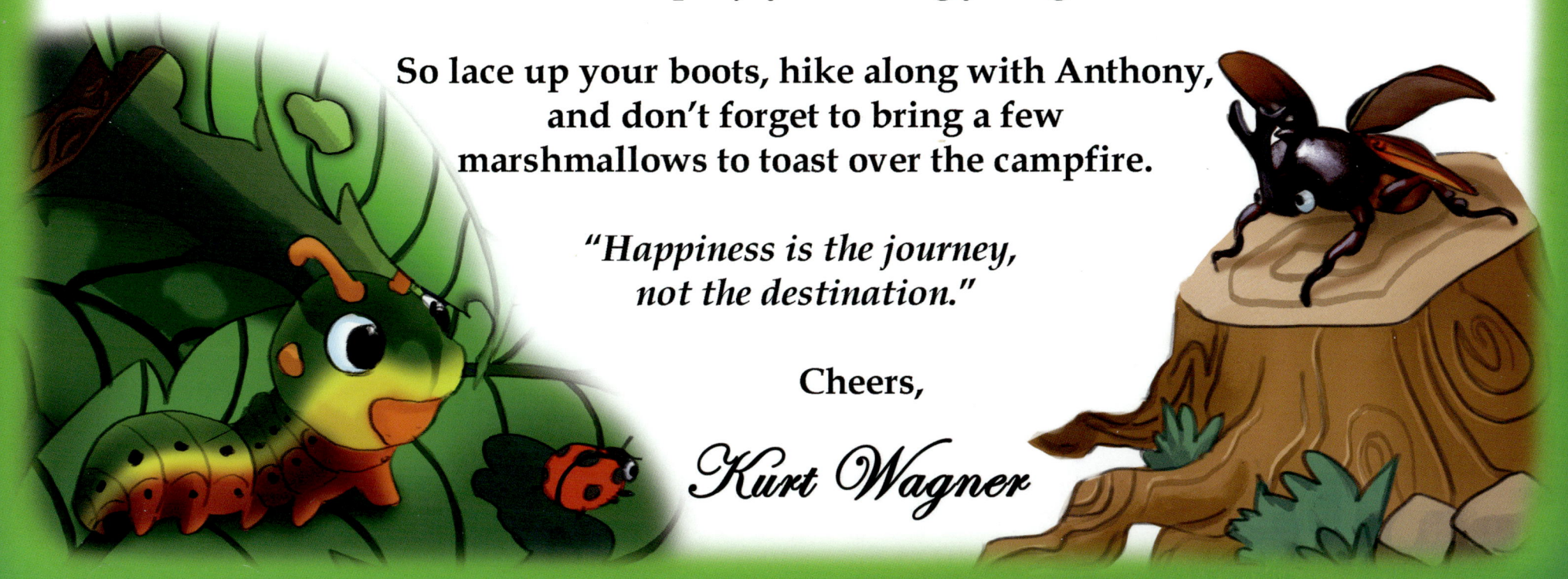

So lace up your boots, hike along with Anthony, and don't forget to bring a few marshmallows to toast over the campfire.

"Happiness is the journey, not the destination."

Cheers,

Kurt Wagner

I would like to thank my wife, Tina, and our children, Jake, Ciarra, Kole, and Alec for their support as we continue creating and adding fun stories to our Anthony's Adventures children's book series.
I feel very blessed to work together as a family on this project and would also like to thank our illustrator, Qing, for her wonderful illustrations that help make our children's books extra special for readers of all ages.

Kurt Wagner

Anthony's Outdoor Adventure

Text Copyright © 2020 by Kurt James Wagner
Illustrations Copyright © 2020 by Kurt James Wagner
All rights reserved. Published by Bee Happy Publishing, Bellevue, Iowa.

No part of this publication may be reproduced, stored in a retrieval system or transmitted in any form or by any means, electronic, mechanical, photocopying, recording, or otherwise, without written permission of the publisher. For information regarding permission, contactus@AnthonyTheMouse.com.

Printed in the United States
Production Date: August 2020
ISBN 978-1-7348198-4-7 (hardcover)
Library of Congress Control Number: 2020913771

Anthony's Outdoor Adventure

Written by
Kurt Wagner and Family

Illustrated by
Qing Yang

Bee Happy Publishing

The early morning sunlight warmed Anthony's fur as he stepped out of his door onto the fireplace mantle. He let out an early morning yawn and stretched his body. *What a perfect day to go for a hike and do some camping!* he thought.

Excited about the day ahead, Anthony scurried to find everything he would need for his outdoor adventure.

He rummaged through storage boxes, checked up in the attic,

and even looked under his bed as he gathered up hiking gear and camping supplies.

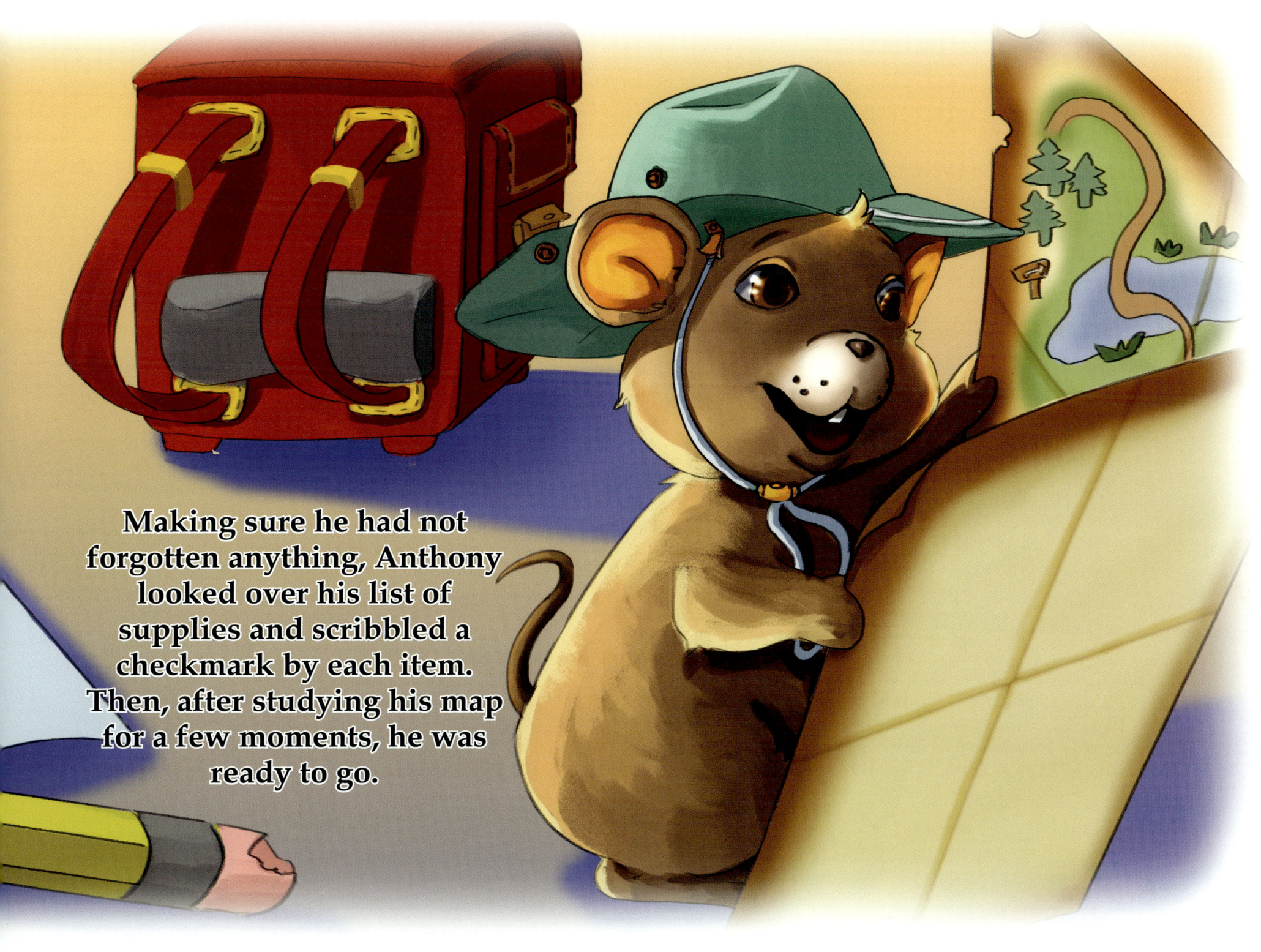

Making sure he had not forgotten anything, Anthony looked over his list of supplies and scribbled a checkmark by each item. Then, after studying his map for a few moments, he was ready to go.

Butterflies fluttered in the morning breeze as Anthony skipped along the meadow's path and hummed a little tune. He saw a caterpillar munching on a leaf and bumble bees buzzing from flower to flower. He noticed a spider clearing the morning dew from her web while tiny ants marched in a row as they carried food back to their anthill.

Walking along the meadow's grassy path, Anthony plucked a dandelion and blew the fluffy seeds into the air. He watched them float away like hundreds of tiny parachutes drifting over the flowery field.

The path led Anthony to a fallen tree log, which he used to cross a narrow stream that emptied into a quiet blue lake.

Once across the stream, he paused to skip a few rocks on the smooth lake water; counting each skip before the rocks sank. Flat rocks made the best skippers.

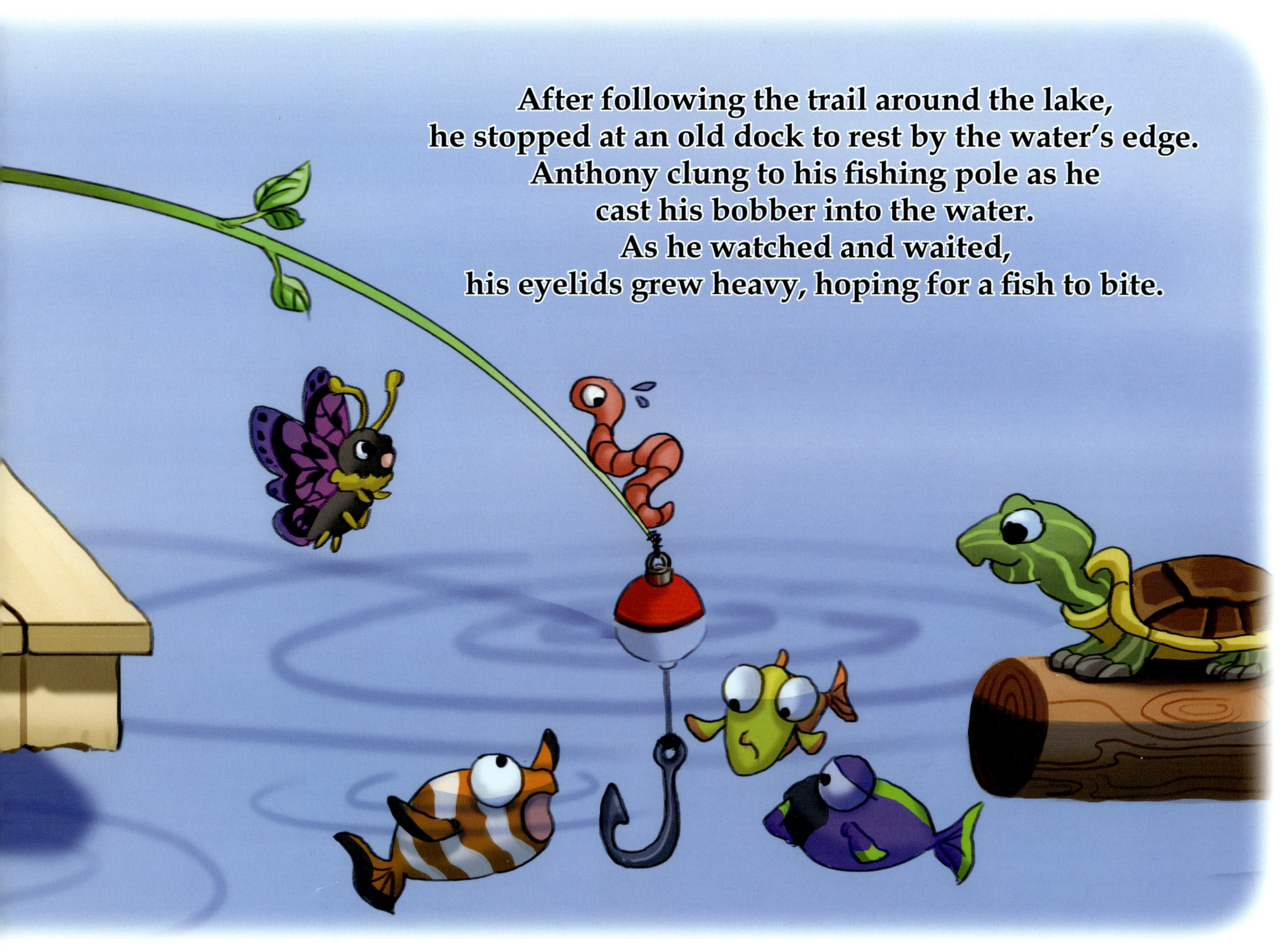

After following the trail around the lake,
he stopped at an old dock to rest by the water's edge.
Anthony clung to his fishing pole as he
cast his bobber into the water.
As he watched and waited,
his eyelids grew heavy, hoping for a fish to bite.

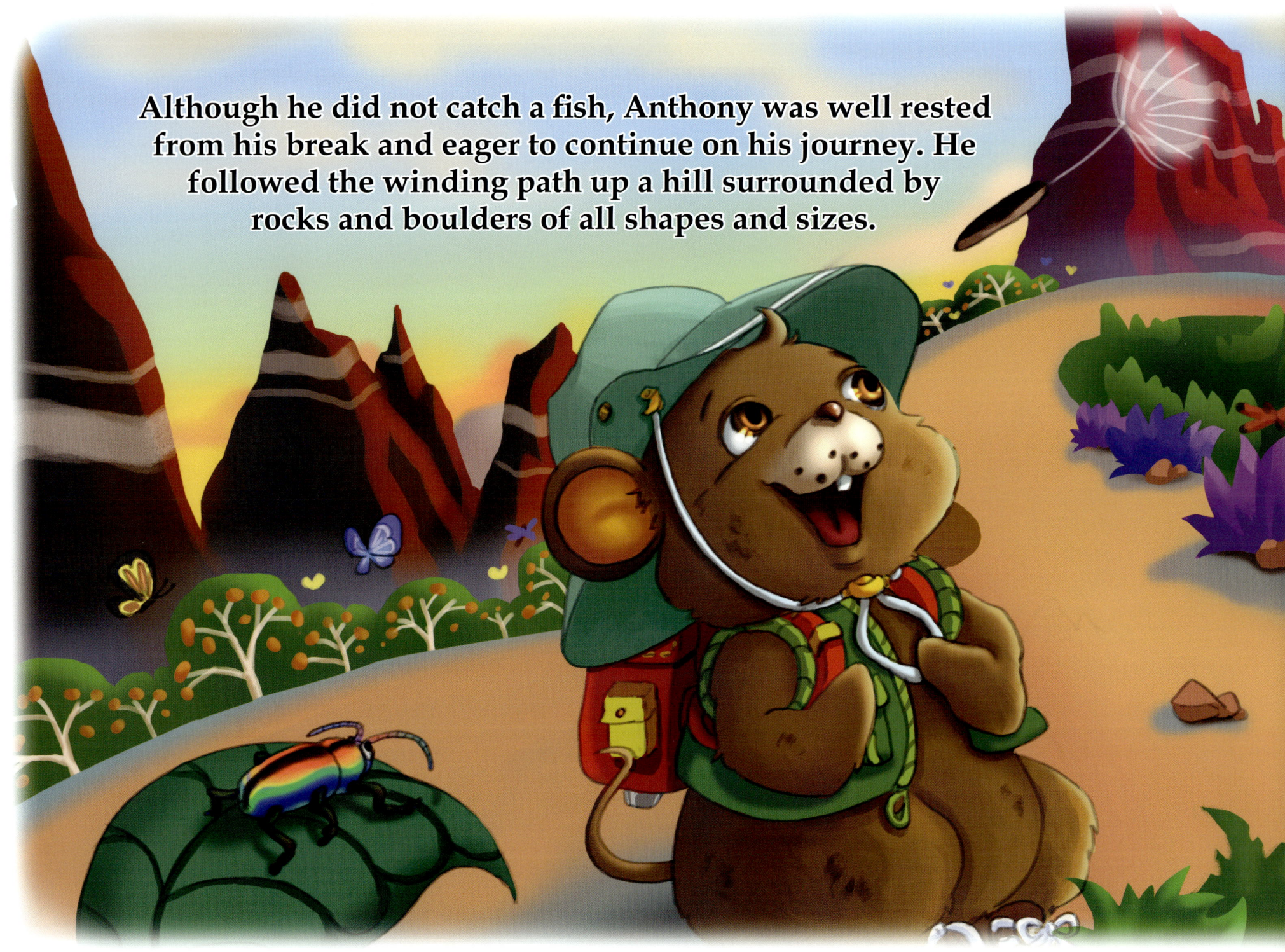

Although he did not catch a fish, Anthony was well rested from his break and eager to continue on his journey. He followed the winding path up a hill surrounded by rocks and boulders of all shapes and sizes.

Straying from the trail for a moment, Anthony climbed up to a rocky ledge that overlooked the canyon below. After pausing to catch his breath, he got out his binoculars. With only a few small clouds dotting the bright blue sky, he could see for miles and miles!

The day was growing warmer as Anthony climbed down from the canyon overlook. The hot sun beat down as he sipped some water from his canteen, quenching his thirst. While drinking, he noticed a small waterfall that would make for the perfect spot to have his picnic lunch.

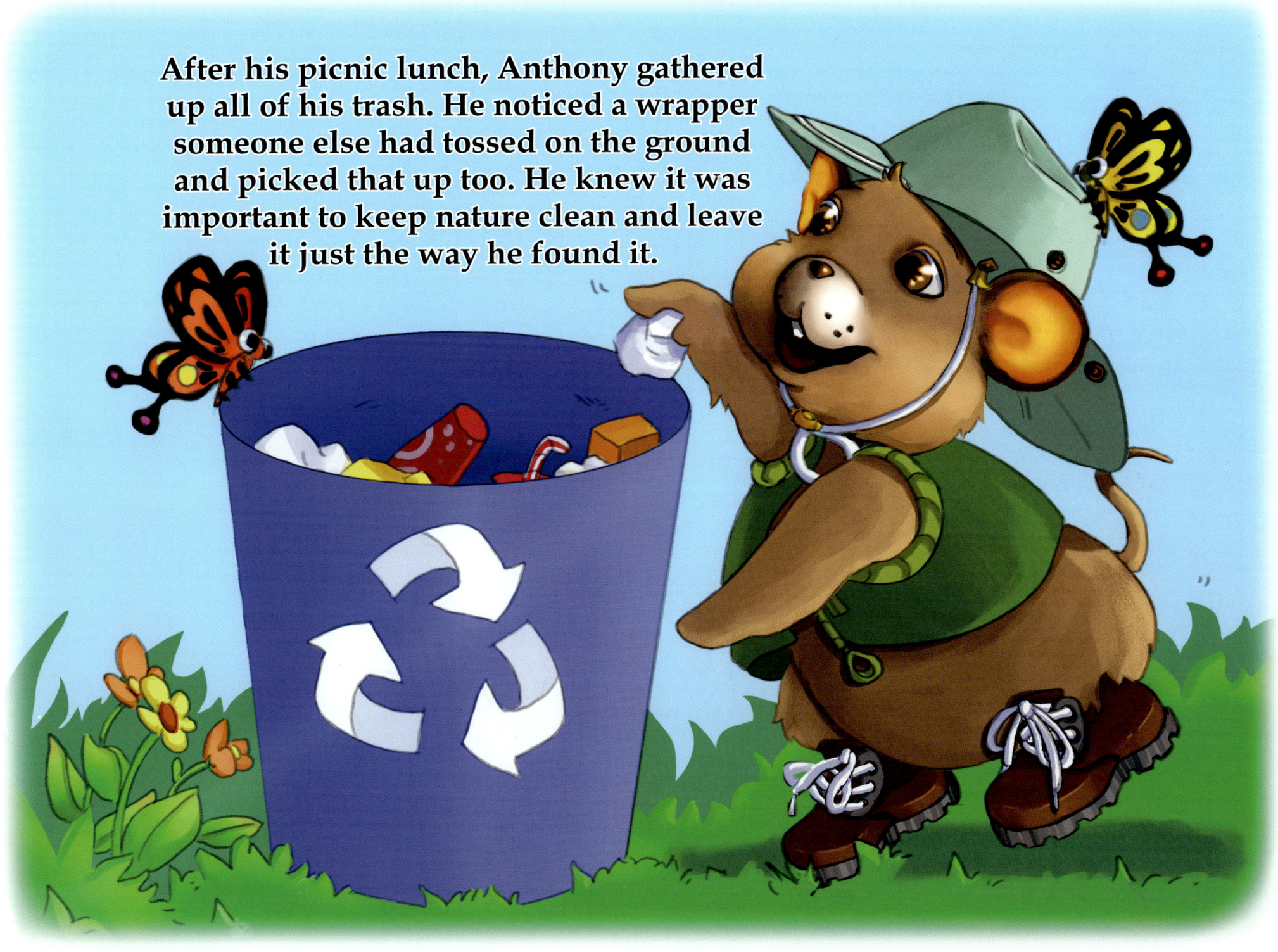

After his picnic lunch, Anthony gathered up all of his trash. He noticed a wrapper someone else had tossed on the ground and picked that up too. He knew it was important to keep nature clean and leave it just the way he found it.

What a great way to cool off on such a hot afternoon, Anthony thought, as he splashed around under the small waterfall that spilled from the canyon rocks.

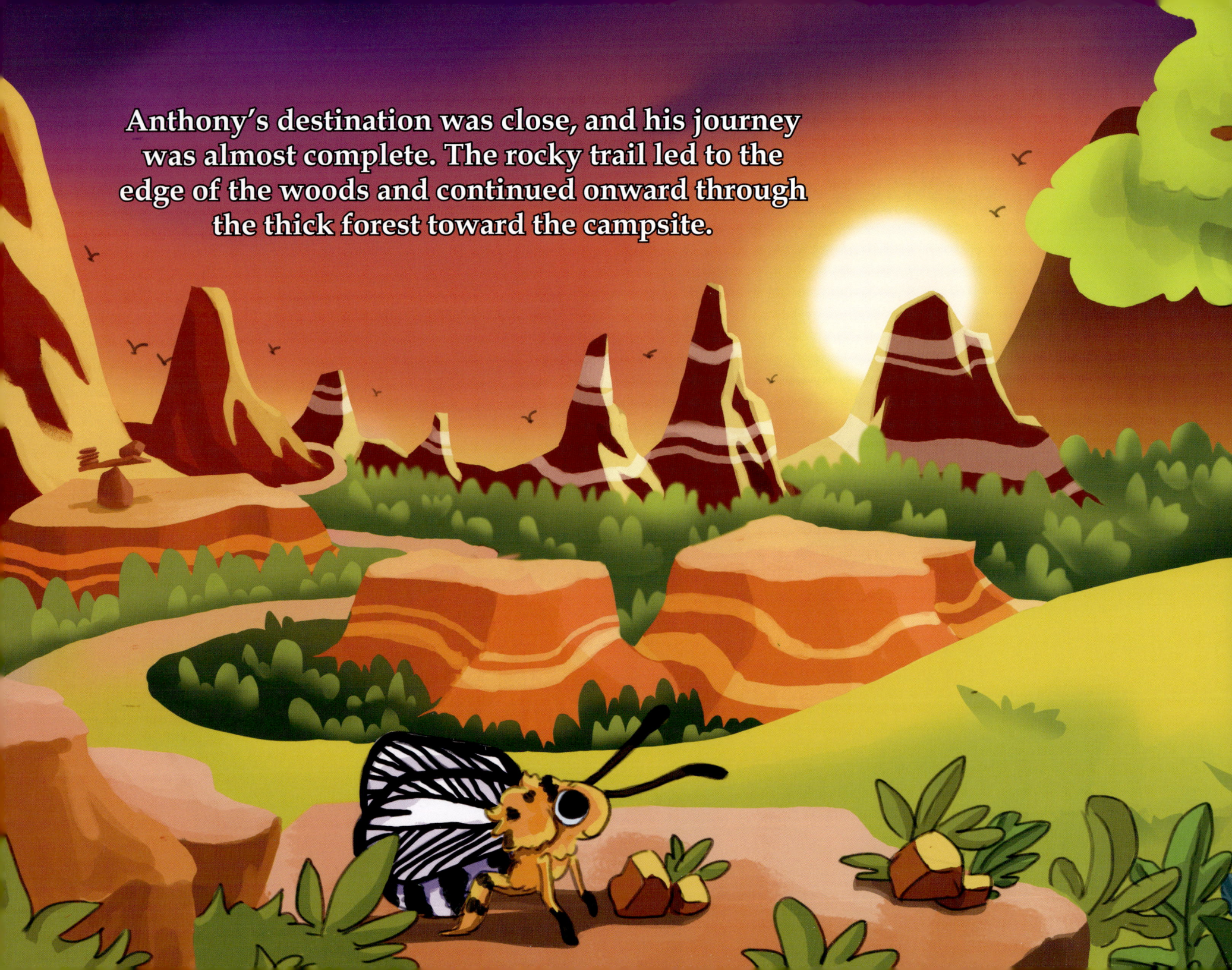

Anthony's destination was close, and his journey was almost complete. The rocky trail led to the edge of the woods and continued onward through the thick forest toward the campsite.

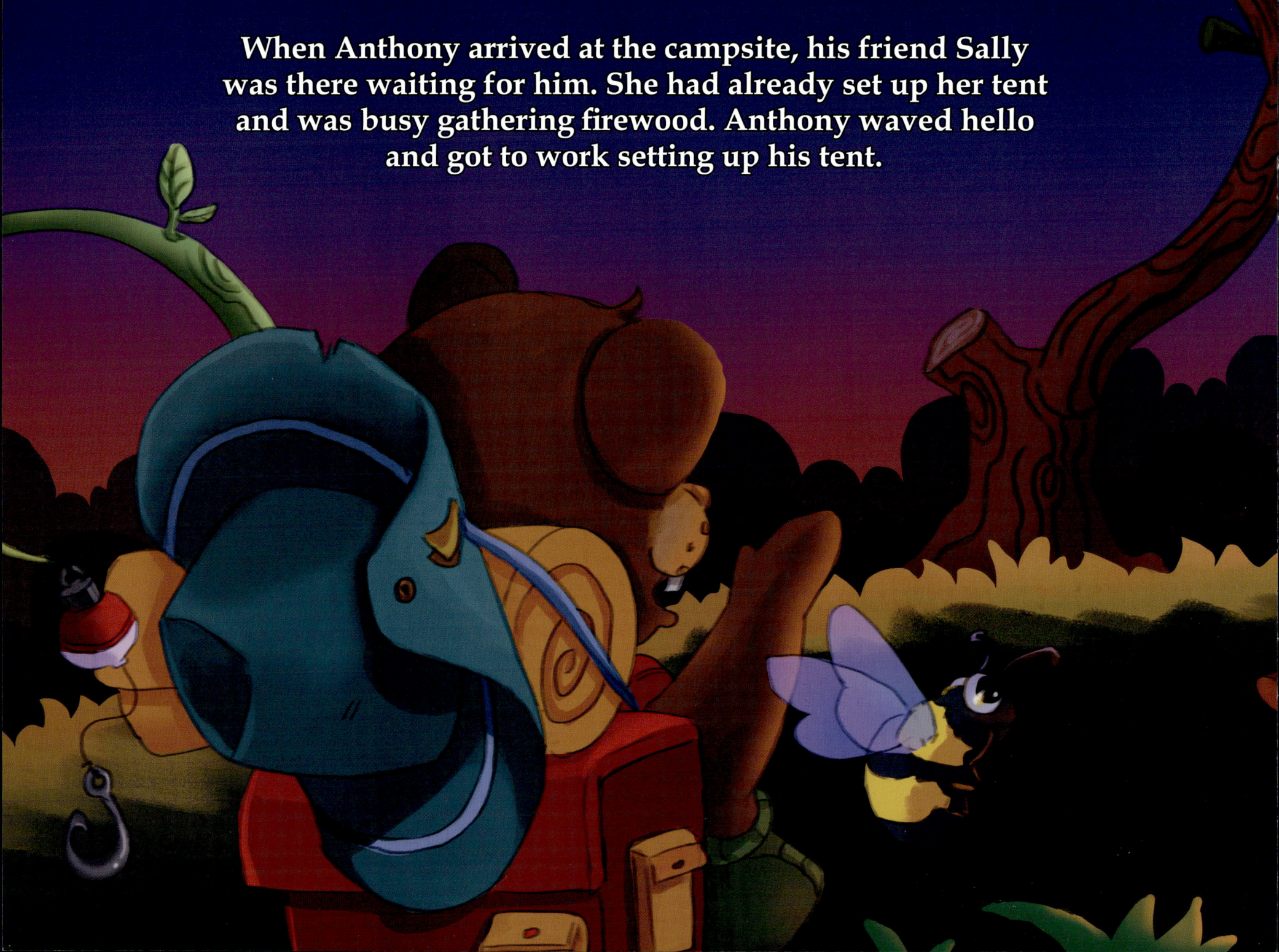

When Anthony arrived at the campsite, his friend Sally was there waiting for him. She had already set up her tent and was busy gathering firewood. Anthony waved hello and got to work setting up his tent.

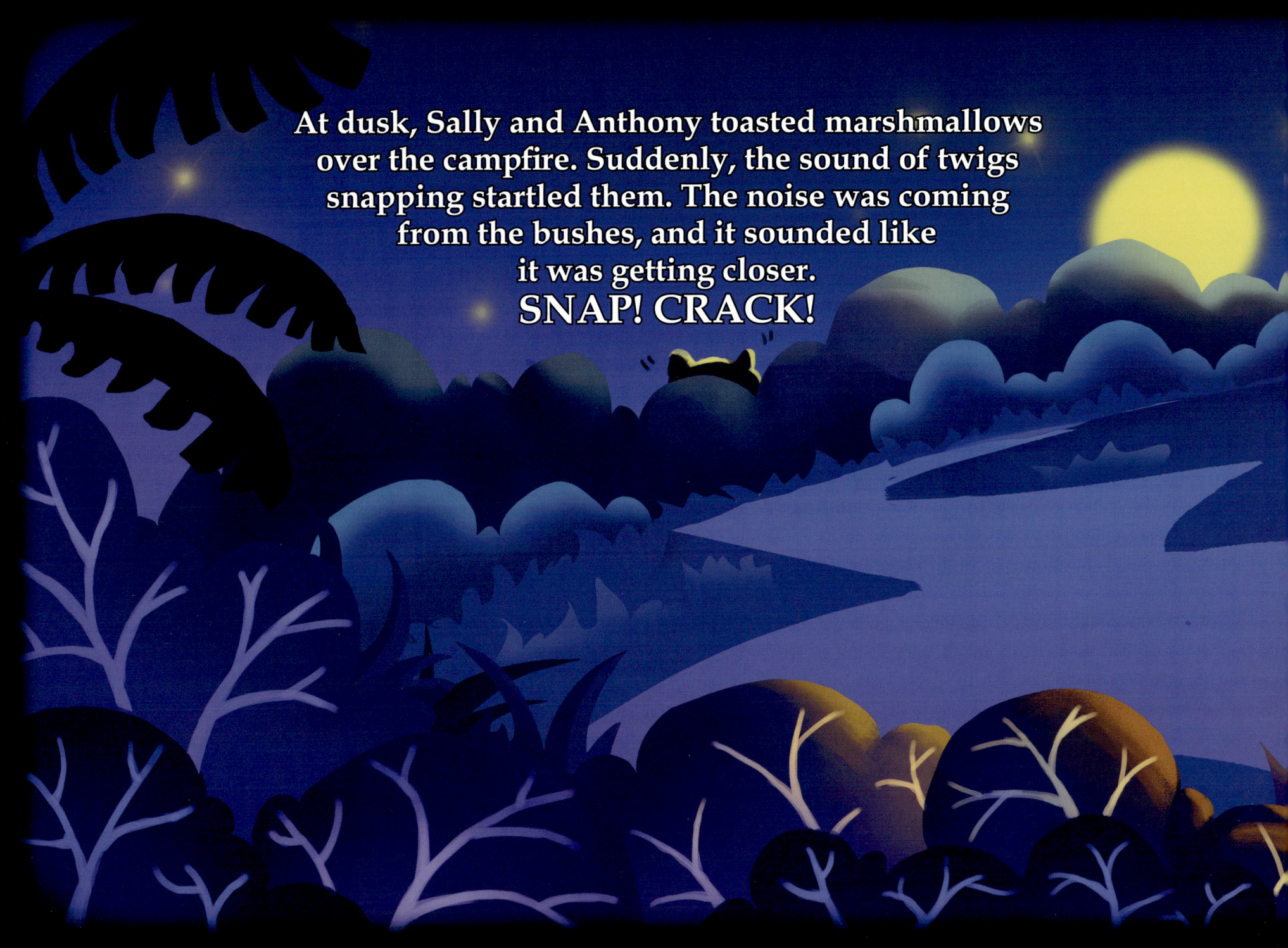

At dusk, Sally and Anthony toasted marshmallows over the campfire. Suddenly, the sound of twigs snapping startled them. The noise was coming from the bushes, and it sounded like it was getting closer.
SNAP! CRACK!

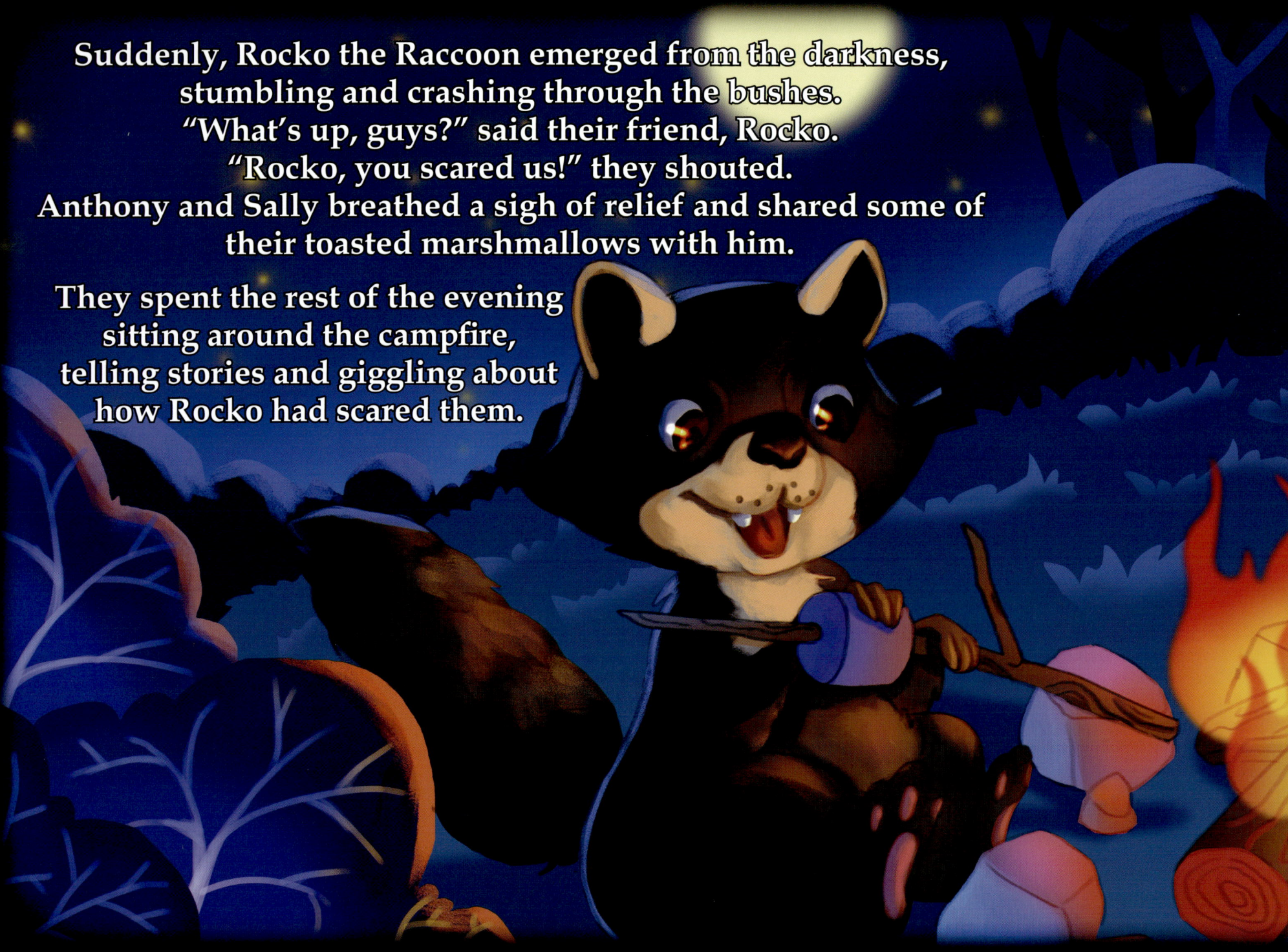

Suddenly, Rocko the Raccoon emerged from the darkness, stumbling and crashing through the bushes.
"What's up, guys?" said their friend, Rocko.
"Rocko, you scared us!" they shouted.
Anthony and Sally breathed a sigh of relief and shared some of their toasted marshmallows with him.

They spent the rest of the evening sitting around the campfire, telling stories and giggling about how Rocko had scared them.

The moon and stars shone brightly as Rocko left for home with a belly full of marshmallows and some very sticky whiskers. Anthony and Sally caught a few fireflies and put them in jars to use for their nightlights before climbing into their tents and going to sleep.

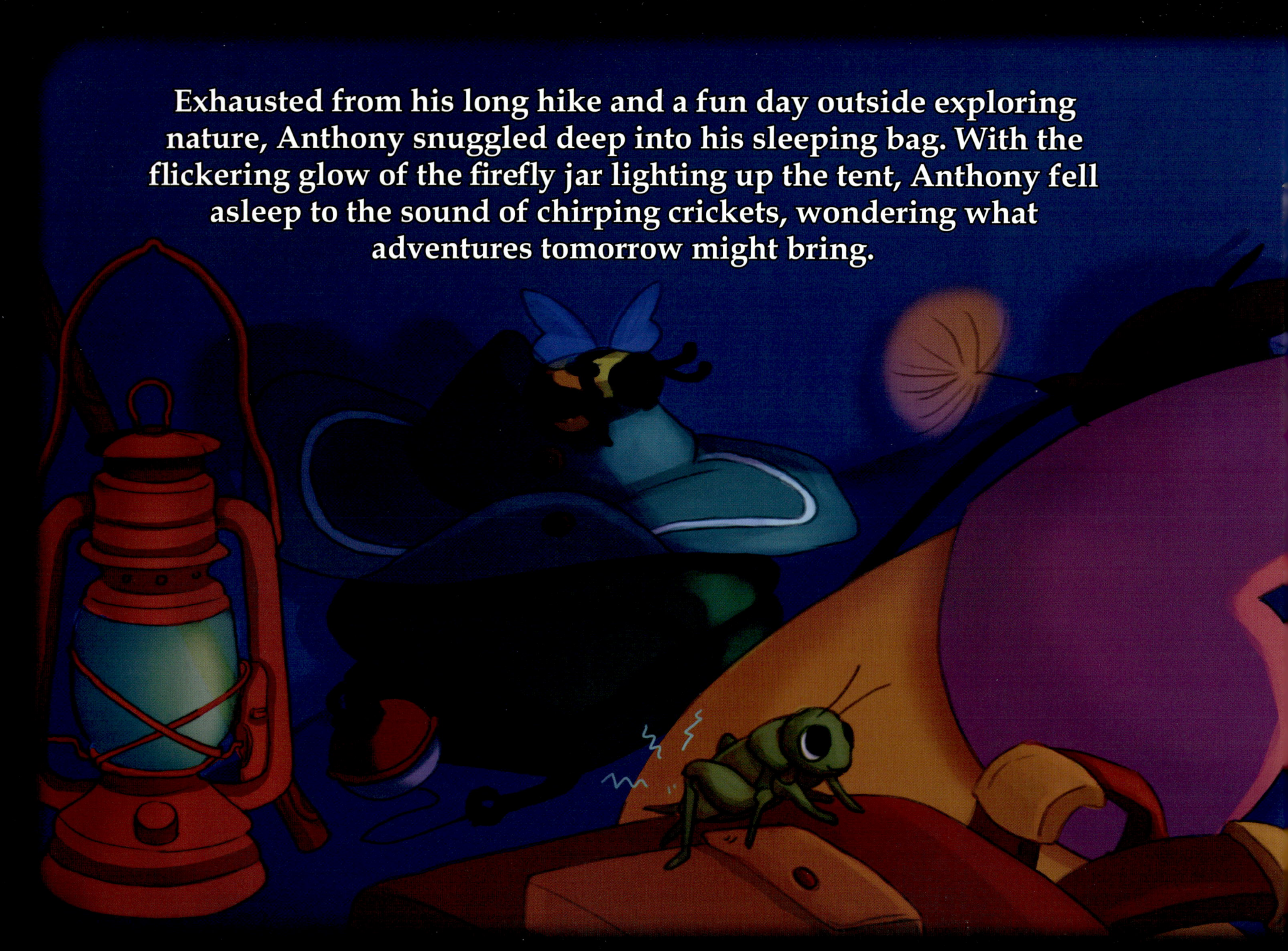

Exhausted from his long hike and a fun day outside exploring nature, Anthony snuggled deep into his sleeping bag. With the flickering glow of the firefly jar lighting up the tent, Anthony fell asleep to the sound of chirping crickets, wondering what adventures tomorrow might bring.

The End